'My Cup Runneth Over'

Lots of Love

Pam

Feb 2011

I'm a Dog
You're a Cat

By Marla Press

Illustrated by Jim Tweedy

Love Lessons From Our Furry Friends

I'm a Dog, You're a Cat
Love Lessons From Our Furry Friends
By Marla Press

Edited by Mark Hiebert & Keystone Resources

Book Design & Layout by Keystone Resources

Printed in the United States of America
Library of Congress Cataloging-in-Publication data

ISBN 978-0-9830968-0-1

Previous books by Jim Tweedy:
"Charlie the RedCat"

First Edition

Dedicated to Dogs & Cats everywhere,
and those they love.

Table of Contents

Introduction 1

Personality Traits of Dogs & Cats 5

Sam & Gabrielle............................... 9

Alexa & Ben 15

Darrell & Lisa 19

Charlie & Marianne 25

Claudia & Bill 31

The Tale of Cats & Dogs 37

Glossary 44

About the Author 46

About the Illustrator 46

Foreword

Once upon a time, I found the most incredible love ever. Alas, we didn't speak the same language. My heart told me I was exactly where I was supposed to be, but my head just could not understand my fabulous new man's behavior.

One day my dear friend, Manisha Thakor, a financial guru who has an uncanny gift for making the complicated seem clear, pointed out that most people are emotionally hard-wired to behave like a dog or a cat. Using her own relationship as an example, she told me how she is an über-cat married to a loyal doggy and how she has maintained a happy marriage.

That's when I realized I was a dog and my significant other was a cat.

She gave me the magic bone every doggy should grab and run with: "Marla, cats just do not love the same way you doggies do. That doesn't mean we don't love, we just don't love in the same way."

Once upon a time, I found the most incredible love ever. Alas, we didn't speak the same language.

"Please don't waste an ounce of energy feeling bad that sometimes your cat goes into emotional hibernation. That's like being annoyed that grass turns brown in the winter. It just does. So comfort yourself in knowing that just as the grass will turn green again, your cat will come back to play with you."

And then, she gave me the power phrase that has become my dog-loves-cat mantra: "Emotional pressure is to a cat what garlic is to a vampire: It's guaranteed to send them away for good!"

As a dog, being able to reach out to Manisha and get her "cat coach" point of view was the emotional equivalent of on-demand scratches behind the ears. Time and again Manisha gave me insight into why my beloved cat was behaving in ways that I, as a doggy, simply could not understand. Using the metaphor of dogs and cats helped me understand situations that my head could not.

That's what I hope this book will do for you. So throw your feet up, grab a bone or your favorite stuffed mouse, and turn the pages to find out if you are a dog or cat ... and learn how to make sure your love keeps coming back.

Introduction

It's a fact that relationships are tough. Sometimes, it feels like we're not even speaking the same language. Very often we're not. There have been thousands of books written, songs sung, and paintings painted around the notion that men and women are different. It's even been claimed that men and women are from different planets.

I argue that men and women are not so different. Rather, people at their core are hard-wired either to be like a dog or a cat.

It's guaranteed: People will drive one another crazy. We do things our loved ones don't expect. Our partners do things that we find completely incomprehensible.

If you're like most people, you drive yourself nuts trying to figure out why the people around you don't act in the ways you expect. Expressed or not, chances are they are thinking the same thing about you! Wouldn't it be wonderful if we all had a language to communicate with those whom we love but don't always understand?

Sometimes, it feels like we're not even speaking the same language.

1

First we must understand ourselves. We don't realize that at our core, we're one of two things: either a dog or a cat.

It's not about gender. It's not about age. It's not about being married or single. It applies to your relationships with your friends, your boss, and your significant other. It's about understanding your *cattitude* or *dogsense*.

The stories are inspired by true friends in real situations. I am grateful they decided to share their experiences in an attempt to help others understand the opposite breed.

"I'm a Dog, You're A Cat: Love Lessons From Our Furry Friends" will help you discover tail-waggin' joy and create purr-fect harmony with the people who drive you crazy. The animal insights on love and how to gain a deeper appreciation of your partner will help you better know yourself and give you tools to understand the dogs and cats in your life.

Cattitude: related to catness, it is expressive of the overall approach cats take to who and what they encounter. It speaks to a degree of assuredness and inner strength that is balanced with a logical, reasoned approach to life.

Dogsense: each decision is principally guided by way of the heart and what each moment presents. It is directly connected to dogiliciousness and upholds a confident, faithful belief that goals will be achieved even when you are unsure how they will happen.

Dogs and cats do things differently. They act differently, think differently, and respond differently. While there may be some overlap in what they like (after all, lap time is always good, as is some good lovin' on the chin or belly), canines and felines value different motivators.

Catness: Descriptive of the coolness of cats. It is a factor of self-sufficiency and occasional aloofness.

Do you want to know who you are? Do you prefer spending the day curled up in a sun-drenched, cushy chair like a cat or is a romp in the grass and mud more your style? When you think there's something in the air, do you sniff it out, or do you just take note, keep an eye open, and stay focused on what seems of paramount importance?

Whether you're a dog or a cat, there's always something to chase. Do you chase it for the fun of the chase, so you can play with what you catch because it's in your territory, or because it needs to know you're the boss?

Why you engage in the pursuit provides the answer about your *catness* or *dogiliciousness.* So who are you?

Dogiliciousness: Fabulousness and excitement define the canine perspective on life, where the world is something into which one should run, dive, and dig with the greatest degree of passion possible. This makes dogs exciting to be around, although it takes a great deal of energy to keep up once a dog gets going.

Dogese: The language of dogs expresses a great degree of passion, although it is somewhat verbose.

Dog

Happy!
Normally needy
Loves lovin'
Tail-wagging joy
Will sniff it out, whatever "it" is
Happy to see you whether you're
  gone for one hour or one year
Speaks *Dogese*
Appreciate me. Now.

Cat

Ambiguous
Occasionally aloof
Satisfactorily assured
"Yes, I'll let you scratch my chin"
The pure embodiment of cattitude
Speaks *Catlish*
Bow down and pet me. Now!

Sam, a dog, is married to Gabrielle, a cat. Gabrielle travels for work and is gone for a few days at a time. Sam also travels for work, almost as often as Gabrielle.

During one particularly busy trip, Gabrielle called home only once. Sam was beside himself with worry and began to panic. His universe was completely out of balance. Being the dog that he is, Sam calls home at least twice a day, sometimes as much as five times when he travels, to speak with his beloved cat.

His universe was completely out of balance.

When Gabrielle finally came home, she found Sam distraught. Before she could set down her bags, he barked, "I was worried! I thought something happened to you!"

In her most sincere cat persona, Gabrielle very nonchalantly said, "I was busy."

Why was this no big deal to Gabrielle but a major calamity for Sam? Because **Gabrielle is a cat and Sam is a dog,** that's why!

Dog

Ready, willing, and able to please.

"Really! Right now. Whatever you want!"

Cat

Isn't really interested in pleasing much of anyone.
"Really. Thank you for not annoying me."

Alexa, a dog, dates Ben, a cat. Ben is an über-cat, meaning that his catlike behavior is exceptionally pronounced. Ben had been going through some very serious family issues, as well as turmoil within his business. To put it mildly, Ben was one hissing mad cat. Alexa, like most sweet doggies wanted to curl up at Ben's feet and just be there for him during this bad time. Ben wanted none of that. In fact, he pulled away.

As luck would have it, Alexa had a "cat coach" to help her get through this rough time. The coach explained to Alexa that when cats are angry, hurt, or frustrated they just want to be left alone. Trying to be there and help, which is what a dog would want, is like pulling the tail of an angry cat - which is a very bad idea!

Why was Ben pushing Alexa away? **Ben is a cat,** that's why!

... when cats are angry, hurt or frustrated they just want to be left alone.

Dog

Needs attention
Wants attention
Craves attention
Loves attention
Any time, all the time!

Cat

Needs attention
Wants attention
Craves attention
Loves attention
Only when they want it!

Darrell is a dog. Lisa, his wife, is a cat. They're adventurous and take thrilling trips to places few dogs and cats will ever visit. They've toured Africa on safaris and trekked through the Australian Outback.

On one recent vacation, Darrell and Lisa took a kayak trip to do some fishing. Because they're independent, they paddled to their destination in individual boats. They enjoyed one another's company and the scenery along the way.

Upon reaching their fishing spot, Darrell donned his wading boots, readied his gear and set out to catch the greatest fish. Casting and reeling, he was hard at work in the hot afternoon sun. He loved every minute, and Lisa loved watching her hard-working Darrell.

The afternoon went on. Darrell looked back at his lovely Lisa and smiled. There she was, propped up in her kayak, looking fashionably cool in her floppy hat and sunglasses while reading a book. Life was sweet.

Of course, a long day spent fishing will make for a tired doggy. Darrell suggested that they head back.

He took the lead, paddling hard. No matter how fun the day had been, the trek back was becoming far more difficult than he had anticipated. Darrell looked back at Lisa and noticed that she was really struggling with the current. Being the good husband (and doggy) that he is, Darrell stopped and suggested that Lisa tie her kayak to his to help her navigate home. Now working twice as hard, Darrell huffed and puffed, paddling upstream.

"By the way, your back sure does look sexy while you're doing that!"

When he finally eased up to breathe he looked back to see his cat, Lisa, laid back, paddle out of the water and eating a granola bar.

Before words could come out of his mouth, Lisa exclaimed, "Boy, I am sure glad I brought this granola bar!"

Darrell almost had to laugh out loud but before he could say anything, she said, "By the way, your back sure does look sexy while you're paddling!" That made Darrell's day.

Why didn't Darrell get mad when Lisa, the cat, seemed completely indifferent to his hard work? **Because he's a dog!**

The dog loves doing the work and being rewarded for it. The cat doesn't recognize a need for action unless it's clear that action must be taken.

22

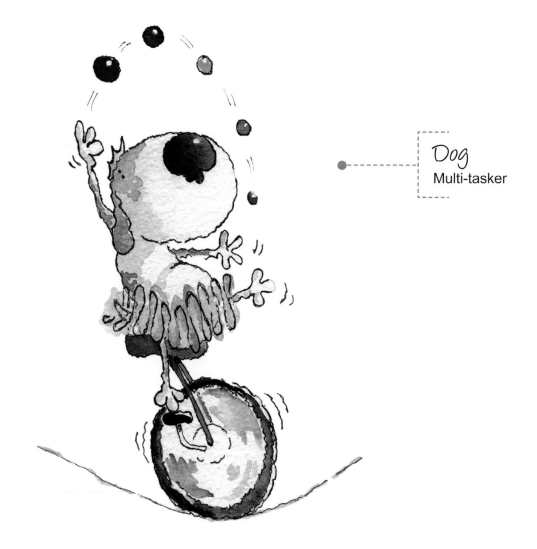

Dog
Multi-tasker

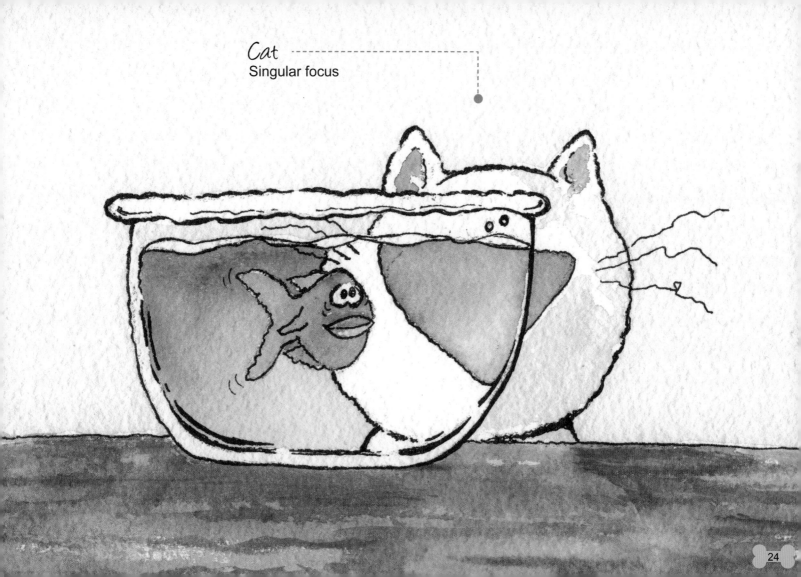

Cat

Singular focus

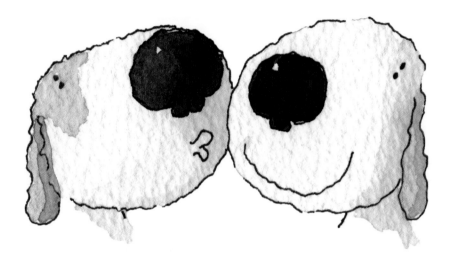

Charlie and his wife Marianne are both Texas dogs. They know they're both dogs because they run in a pack and they wouldn't have it any other way.

One weekend, Charlie and the couple's two Labradors, real dogs named Laura and Dubya, went to their ranch while Marianne stayed home in the city.

It was a big day on the ranch. There were fences to mend, things to smell
and critters to chase. As evening arrived, Charlie and the dogs cooked dinner
and set about relaxing.

It was pleasant to spend a quiet evening in the country so when a phone rings,
it punctuates the night like headlights on a farm road.

Being the dog that she is, Marianne called Charlie five times just to see what they were doing. Charlie understood that she missed her pack and answered each of the calls. He was happy to hear her voice.

Two weeks later, Marianne took the dogs to the ranch and Charlie was the lone city dog. He called Marianne and the dogs numerous times to find out what they were doing without him. He missed his pack.

Why in the world would Charlie and Marianne behave this way? **Because they are dogs,** that's why!

Dogs need one another. It is psychologically important for them to know that everyone in the pack is okay. Cats don't have that same need.

Dog - •

Pack animal. Prefers to be around
people (those he cares for).

Cat

Independent. Prefers to be alone
(unless he doesn't want to be alone).

Claudia, a cat, is married to Bill, a big and busy dog. On most days before Bill heads out for work, he will post little yellow sticky notes that express his feelings for Claudia in random and surprising places.

One day, she found a note with "I love you" attached to her toothpaste tube. Another note greeted her at the refrigerator that said, "Have a wonderful day, Sunshine!"

Unlike most cats, Claudia enjoys taking long showers. When finishing her shower one morning, she got out to find a "You are beautiful" note posted to the mirror.

When Claudia reads the notes, she sighs sweetly and promptly tosses them away.

It might have been the only time Claudia had ever done such a thing.

One day, when Claudia was leaving town for several days, she thought she would do something sweet for Bill. She left him a yellow sticky note on his briefcase that said "I love you." It might have been the only time Claudia had ever done such a thing. After all she showed her love in other ways

Several months passed. As was their custom, Claudia opened Bill's wallet to get some money. To her surprise, she found the same sticky note she had written to Bill. She took it out, showed it to him and laughed, "Why in the world do you still have this?"

Bill is a dog, and that gesture was important to him, that's why!

While cats and dogs are both loving and loyal, dogilicious passions involve some sentimentality: Like old bones or a good chew toy, the things around us have as much meaning as actions and words.

Cats may have things they like, too, like the scratching post or a favorite spot in the sun, but a cat isn't generally going to play with the same toy day after day.

Dog

Loving and loyal
Overt
Robust
Sentimental
Keeps mementos

Cat
Loving and loyal
Subtle
Delicate
Unattached
"Who needs mementos
   when you have memories?"

The Tale of Cats & Dogs

Here's the secret to a good relationship: Learn to understand the motives of the person you are communicating with so that you can speak his or her language. Like foreign languages, meanings arrive by different terms and accents. Two expressions that look like they should mean the same thing sometimes have very different meanings.

As a dog, I understand my cat, über cat that he is: When he behaves in a certain way, it generally has nothing to do with me and mostly has to do with his "cat ways."

I believe the same holds true for the cats who are dealing with us doggies. For instance, it may drive you crazy when your companion prances through the day, wagging his or her tail. However, if you understand doggies are just hard-wired that way, then you can let them play and frolic all day long while you tend to your very important cat things.

The real question is: Does a dog-with-cat relationship work and more importantly, why?

... there is nothing more aggravating than having someone around who is even happier or more excited than you!

Let's look at the relationship with two dogs. While this can work, it's not a given. Dogs are pack animals and there always needs to be a leader in the pack. Obviously, if you are a dog, then you know you are supposed to be the leader. Never mind the other dog in the relationship.

Dogs tend to have a superhero's focus on pleasing their loved ones, which also means that dogs need reassurance. As a result, when it's dog with dog, there tends to be too much neediness for a healthy relationship. As a dog, there is nothing more aggravating than having someone around who is even happier or more excited than you!

What about two cats? Have you ever seen cats run in a pack? If a cat marries a cat, over time there becomes so much ambivalence that nobody really cares. Finally, everyone just yawns and says, "Meh."

Finding our opposite fulfills something that we clearly lack in ourselves.

Differences create good things, and everyone thinks it's so cute when they see a picture of a happy cat and a happy dog together.

In many ways, dog-and-cat relationships are the strongest. They address each other's weaknesses: Sometimes making the most of life takes cat claws. Sometimes it takes a dog's fangs. Sometimes canine strength carries the day and sometimes feline agility gets us where we want to be.

Finding our opposite fulfills something that we clearly lack in ourselves. The trick is knowing what you are, what your partner is, and what your partner thinks you are. Once that is learned, you will know the exact spot to scratch and how to keep the claws and teeth in check.

When you learn *Catlish* and *Dogese*, you can translate difficult situations and conversations into positive, nurturing, and enriching results.

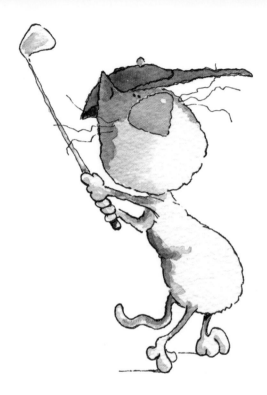

If you know your doggy is feeling unloved or under-appreciated, rather than engaging in a conversation about "feelings," you can just provide a scratch behind the ear, a good game of catch, or one of those extra-special treats.

When your cat is feeling overwhelmed and says he needs to spend some time in his "cat cave," just let him go hit a couple of balls, and you go run with your pack for the next few days.

At the end of the day, I wouldn't want it any other way. I love my cat and appreciate that I may one day become a little more catlike and independent. My hope is that someday he becomes a bit more doglike ... but I'm not crossing my paws on that one!

Glossary

Catness   Descriptive of the coolness of cats. It is a factor of self-sufficiency and occasional aloofness.

Catlish   The language of cats is characterized by a strong degree of logic and a certain amount of verbal economy. This means much can be expressed in a concise manner.

Cattitude   Related to Catness, it is expressive of the overall approach cats take to who and what they encounter. It speaks to a degree of assuredness and inner strength balanced with a logical, reasoned approach to life. The intent to use others to serve their own needs.

Dogese   The language of dogs expresses a great degree of passion although it is somewhat verbose.

Dogilicious   Fabulousness and excitement define the canine perspective on life, where the world is something into which one should run, dive and dig with the greatest degree of passion. This makes dogs exciting to be around although it takes a great deal of energy to keep up with them.

Dogsense   Each decision is principally guided by way of the heart and what each moment presents. It is directly connected to dogiliciousness and upholds a confident, faithful belief that goals will be achieved even when you are unsure how they will happen.

About the Author: Marla Press

Marla Press was born and raised in Rock Island, Illinois. She attended the University of Illinois, Champaign-Urbana and graduated with a bachelor of science degree in communications-advertising from the University of Texas at Austin before starting her career in the financial services industry.

The book series "I'm a Dog, You're a Cat" was born out of trying to understand a new relationship in her life. When Marla shared the idea with her new "über-kitty," he thought the concept was so great he offered his full support – a big, huge deal for a cat! Thus came the idea for the book.

Marla lives in Houston, Texas with her two real rescue dogs, Riley and Bella.

About Illustrator: Jim Tweedy

Jim Tweedy, born in the late 1950s in Covington, Louisiana, began his artistic journey at an early age. From childhood art lessons with his father and former Disney animator, Byron Tweedy, to studying under famed former NASA illustrator, Walter Labiche, Jim developed his talents into a way of life.

In May 1992, Jim found his fame with Charlie the RedCat. In 2002, Jim realized that "man cannot live by cat alone" and created Jim Tweedy's Friendly Doggies. These cartoon dogs are humorous and endearing, and have captured the hearts of animal lovers and art collectors alike.